THE COMING THING

Martina Evans is an Irish poet and novelist and the author of twelve books of prose and poetry. *American Mules* (Carcanet, 2021) – was a *TLS* and *Sunday Independent* (Ireland) Book of the Year. It won the 2022 Pigott Poetry Prize. She is a books critic for the *Irish Times*.

The Coming Thing

MARTINA EVANS

CARCANET POETRY

The author gratefully acknowledges the Royal Literary Fund for its assistance.

First published in Great Britain in 2023 by
Carcanet
Alliance House, 30 Cross Street
Manchester, M 2 7 A Q
www.carcanet.co.uk

A CIP catalogue record for this book is
available from the British Library.

ISBN 978 1 80017 345 3

Book design by Andrew Latimer, Carcanet
Typesetting by LiteBook Prepress Services
Printed in Great Britain by SRP Ltd, Exeter, Devon

The publisher acknowledges financial
assistance from Arts Council England.

For Dora and Donny

My mama says I'm a mistake.
    That I made her a bad girl.
My playhouse is underneath
  Our house, & I hear people
    Telling each other secrets.

Yusef Komunykaa, Venus Fly-traps

Some children are cherished more than others.

Derek Scally, The Best Catholics in the World

THE COMING THING

1.

JUSTIN said I'd been seen passing a joint on Patrick's Bridge
when I thought I was pure invisible. Escaped. But sure
Knocklong was only twelve miles away. Johnny O'Hare turned
up at a Twenty-First party on Coburg Street – two
thirty-one-year-olds were holding it, ten years late. He said,
Hello Imelda! & I said, *I don't know you*, & turned my back
in my wet-look yellow anorak under the navy sky.
Drowning out home, holding seánces with red-haired Donny &
Dora & Carl near Wilton shopping centre. When Science
became a stranger to me, boiling panic took root.
Cork city & Knocklong merged. When one was above ground,
the other creaked underfoot. Justin's black tar eyes running
everywhere, *"I'll be judge, I'll be jury," said cunning old Fury.*

2.

SOMEONE was singing about not knowing much about
a Science Book. *And what about the French she took?*
Ah she's good at French, Agnes said when I walked in
on herself & Justin roasting mushrooms on the range.
You'd want to keep away from the mushrooms! Justin said
when he saw me. *Have you seen the size of you? Ah no,*
said Agnes. *But remember when she took up Domestic Science
& dropped the toast in the poached egg water?* I remembered
dropping red-hot shortbread fingers, scraping dough off
the cracked blue lino, Justin standing over me. His black
eyes. *Domestic Science, how are you!* Turning the other cheek,
I said, *But I do know that I love you,* & Justin said, *You've
lost the fecking plot.* And I said, *But that's the chorus of the
song you were singing. What song?* said Agnes.

3.

JUSTIN said he'd heard I'd dissected a shark with
a handkerchief over my face. Did I think I was
the Ned Kelly of Science? *But Ned Kelly had
his head in a bucket!* Justin said I could write
that down, *I hear you're hanging around with a cheap
crowd!* Old Johnny O'Hare asked in the shop what was
I doing in Cork & Justin said *sweet fuck all* & Old Johnny
O'Hare said, *Oh right so, I'll have Twenty Carrolls & a
box of red matches.* Drove off fast in his powder blue
Cortina. *And he's a fucking wife killer,* said Justin, looking
after him. *You can see his beard growing while he's talking
to you!* Agnes said she said nothing. It hurt her to the
quick *to be even asked.* But someone was giving Justin
information. Like in a police state.

4.

DORA'S fierce intellectual, I said. But where did I think
she'd get a job with *Arts*? Justin wanted to know. He
made Arts sound like farts. After I doing Science to be
sensible like Agnes! *She's a bloody female engineer,*
can you believe it? Justin said. I wanted to be unbelievable too.
But it wasn't like school where Sister Joseph's wooden table
was clean, dry, stacked with sheets of pictures of brains &
hearts to be coloured in. Like Holy Pictures, venous blue
& arterial red. Notes on the Reproductive System
handed out silently. No stinking. No dripping. No
dogfish. That desperate army of *Jaws*. Was it even fair
to them? Should they be slaughtered for our education?
I'm thinking about that, too, like, said Dora.

5.

DORA said she'd go straight to England if she ever got
in Trouble. She was the youngest of ten & a mistake
& when the priest visited her family, he was bent over,
red with laughing, pointing, *Look at the Mistake!*
Hasn't she grown into a fine strong girl! There wasn't enough
love to go around & only a fool would expect it. Dora was
a Utilitarian. She said there had to be population control.
Like for cats. People couldn't go on reproducing themselves
like they were only brilliant like & they were never objective
about their own blue-eyed boys. *What's the first thing a traveller*
will tell a married woman when she sits down in her caravan to have
her fortune told? Your daughter will be successful in catering & your
son will rise to the top of whatever it is!

6.

HOW did some people always know what to do, like?
Dissect a rabbit, cut a plant cross-section for a slide. Poach
eggs & make shortbread. *Silver Spoons & Confidence from Birth,*
said Dora. *Isn't it awful to think there might be no justice?*
I worried along with Dora. Will the first shall be last?
We didn't know. We knew nothing. *Just don't add to the
population in the Name of God!* Dora said & I said I hadn't a
notion of it. I could hardly support *myself* studying
the wrong thing. But Justin wouldn't let me do Arts. I had
to do Science & after that it was supposed to be Computer
Science because that was the coming thing. But really he'd
prefer I did nursing, which was the steadiest job of all.
I'll keep telling you 'til I'm blue in the face!

7.

GET a bank loan! said Justin & his face was scarlet not blue.
But I am sure I am on the wrong course! Justin cut me off,
Anyone who comes along chopping and changing has no character,
no backbone. His Third Wife Clodagh told me to go easy
on the studying because I was so highly-strung & Agnes
said Arts was bad for the nerves. *Nerves!* shouted Justin.
No one with Nerves could be that fat. Old Danny Boy has
Real Depression & he's like a pull-through for a rifle.
Coming home with blown-up eyes like an addict after
you've been seen passing a joint on Patrick's Bridge.
But it was only a rollie washed down with a bottle of Benylin
because of the desperate cough I got when I hit the
blue Gitanes after I left the convent. & that's why I had
to go for the Benylin— for the tickly cough.

8.

JUSTIN thought he was the only man in the world
with a pain or an ache & he was always rolling
up the leg of his trousers to show me the fat blue
branches of his varicose veins snaking around his hairy
red leg. *Look at that!* he said. *And I'm not even fat –*
giving me a disgusted tarry-black look as if I was the
one who should have varicose veins. *How many weeks
did Seán Mac Stíofáin last on hunger strike? & you can't even get
between breakfast & lunch without a pop?* I was sure that
I must be the only girl in Ireland to be subjected to that
kind of leg display by her father. Dora thought she must
be the only child in Ireland to be tormented about being
a mistake by a priest so in a way we were thinking we were
extraordinary too. That's youth for you. It doesn't last long.

9.

WHAT happened to young Johnny O'Hare? said Justin at the
weekend as I was filling my rucksack with packets
of Erin Oxtail Soup. He called Johnny & his sister Greta
The Missing Links & they annoyed him now. *What's up with the
weird glamour?* Johnny wearing navy-blue suits, going round
with videotapes under his arm, *holding forth to fools at
the church wall,* Sundays after Mass. *He's after getting the name of
being a Big Reader. What's that about?* said Justin when Danny Boy
leant up against the counter, his red casino shirt open in a v &
I couldn't believe I ever fancied him. Danny said Johnny read
every single one of Harold Robbins's books & they're that thick!
Thick is right, said Justin. *I remember when the O'Hares had nothing
& were black and blue from Old Johnny's beatings.
Sure, they hardly went to school.*

10.

BIG sisters were everywhere. I was avoiding Carl's sister
Noreen the night The Beat & the Specials came to the Arc.
Even hippies like Dora came. Or maybe I dragged her in her
pale blue skirt & white ankle socks & I was afraid there
would be remarks but no one even noticed her clothes. The sky
was the colour of petrol, everyone on Pondies & cider, screaming &
gobbing lime-green phlegm on MacCurtain Street. Three-feet
high letters flaming red above our heads – *Arcadia Ballroom.*
Everyone calling everyone else *poxy* & then The Beat were *on.*
In Cork. No one could credit it. Everyone was pogoing. But
when I jumped, I thought I saw the top of Noreen's head
so then I stayed down. Carl took off his jumper & I wished
he hadn't because I had a thing against flesh, especially sweating
flesh & I secretly thought gobbing was pure disgusting.

11.

WHEN The Specials came on, the whole of Cork was
roaring that someone was doing *too much too young, getting
married with a kid when they should be having fun &* Noreen
appeared to me behind Dora's back in a flare of nostrils wearing
bubble-gum pink. She said Carl breathed heavily through his nose.
You never noticed, like? She didn't know how I could stand it &
she had no mercy because she didn't want me with Carl. She put
her hand on the back of his neck & looked at me to see how I liked
it. She was doing the Dip, getting ready for the bossing of generations
but there she was too because that was the night, even teachers
were there. Dora was sick in a corner, wiping her face with
the hem of her steel-blue 1940s coat. Terry Hall swayed in
his tartan trousers, asking if we'd heard of the starving millions.
Or contraception.

12.

TOM drove down Patrick's Hill fast in his red Volks
after & we were singing *Anarchy in UK*, delighted with
ourselves except I wasn't really. Tom left the handbrake
off halfway down the steepest hill in Ireland. It was like a funfair.
Where I never had one bit of fun in my whole life. I thought
we were shooting to our deaths on Patrick's Bridge. I could
taste the brown water of the Lee in my mouth. Clinging to the
leather strap like Clodagh did when Justin drove the Mini
in a temper, I pretended to laugh but Dora didn't have to
impress anyone. Best with his shaved head & black & yellow
wasp fringe meant nothing to her. She didn't see the way Tom
wore his father's trousers was avant-garde, that he wasn't
following the crowd. She screamed she was going to be sick
if he didn't *calm down with the fucking driving, like!*

13.

CARL'S black sheet-of-plastic raincoat rattled against me,
his pine-needle breath, still perfect then. When we were back
on the flat, Tom tore the gears across the ground. I thought
the tarmac of Washington Street would split open & as we
passed The Millwheel, three men came out & looked after
us. Tom swerved into the Shell station on Western Road. Dora leapt
out to vomit into blue flower beds & Carl said she was like
a cat with a fur ball & the petrol pump fellow had a face on him
inside of his crimson duffle. He was like something out
of *The Masque of the Red Death* & when Tom said, *Three-fifty*.
he roared *Three-fifty what?* out of the red hood *&* Tom said
Jesus Christ, it's all I've got. Best whispered, *Please, say please. That's
Jimmy Barry, he's dangerous!* Tom said *please* & then when Jimmy
Barry said, *Certainly, sir!* that was even worse.

14.

I HAD to get a bag of Fox's Fruits & I was terrified the way
the red door creaked & the Volks gave a fierce bounce as
I got out & I was creeping past Jimmy who was bent over
the petrol tank when he said from under his arm, *Jesus Christ,
what the fuck are you?* I said I was a punkette & he said, *You are
in your hole, you old culchie. Did ye ever hear of a punk with a country
accent?* & then he said, *Gob, there on the ground so, sure!* I walked
away trembling. I was composing myself at the grille getting my Fox's Fruits
& a bag of chocolate tools – you could buy saws and hammers
& drills all made out of chocolate, they were selling them loose for bargain
prices—when I heard the shouts. The smell of petrol was so strong,
I thought I was at home in Knocklong & Jimmy Barry was holding the nozzle
to Best's head, his steel toes flashing in the orange streetlight, *Where's your
anarchy now?*

15.

TOM jumped out first to defend me, they told me afterwards,
Best followed & then Jimmy pounced like a panther. Carl said
he'd wanted to get out too only no one would let him.
It all happened in slow motion like – the very same as the
machine gun attack in The Wild Bunch. But everyone was pure
terrified no matter what they said. Best was led to the tap
by Dora. She held his eyelids open & Tom splashed them with
water & Jimmy Barry laughed under the red Shell letters.
Hailstones hammered the roof of the Volks as we drove away, Dora's
face violet in the light, Best's hand over his eyes,
me eating a chocolate saw, wondering what anarchy
really meant. Carl said the stinging of petrol was fierce & that
I was a top notch punkette & that Jimmy Barry was
only jealous of Best. *Jealous of what like?* said Dora, sarcastically.

16.

DORA lined the orange spines of her Penguins against our blue
wall in Palace Place View. Two huge rooms for a tenner
a week & a view of the episcopal palace. The landlord came up
from Schull, singing, *The violets were scenting the woods, Nora,*
displaying their charms to the bees! We didn't know where to look
& then he stopped with a big red face & asked us where
the *lolly* was. We were just relieved the song was over. After
he went with his two fivers, I couldn't stop singing, *The violets*
were scenting the woods, Dora! & Dora said *Lolly* was a problem.
But she was after getting her grant money. Like an independent
millionaire. Justin didn't pass the means test so I got nothing.
Agnes said I must never speak about it because Justin
was blue in the face from the Overheads but I just wanted
to be Dora, independent, doing Arts without the farts.

17.

PONDIES were Pondrex, slimming tablets for women. They
sent the girls into the chemists. Twenty in a packet
for one pound twenty. In MacSweeneys, Patrick Street, the
woman came out from behind her counter in her starched
white coat, her moon-blue curls, looked me up and down as I held
my breath, *Have you ever thought of exercise?* I said, *ain't
you heard of the starving millions? &* she said I should be
certified & I was nearly crying when I arrived in the Teach Beag
with no tablets. Carl said take no notice & that I was
only perfect & Tom came up behind him & said *You'll say
anything to* & I ran into the bathroom before
I heard the end of whatever it was, stood there shivering
under my white hair looking into the fluorescent
mirror, my face yellow, purple patches under my sad eyes.

18.

THE Zoology demonstrator carried an electric
blue plastic bath with the stiff, rubbery mouths of the dogfish
pointing upwards, looking humiliated. The stink of
formaldehyde, disgusting picky work, tiny weak veins
to be whittling. Why did nobody mind? They laughed as if
they knew all along. I'd been scientific, reciting
equations, drawing diagrams, twelve colouring pencils.
Happy, clean & dry now everything stank wetly. The veins
went to mush. The fellow with the glasses tried to help but
after a while his navy enlarged eyes avoided mine.
In the end, I stood by the carcase, a white handkerchief
around my hand, pure beaten down like a prisoner of war.
The demonstrator was as disgusted as I was &
I did not think I was Ned Kelly.

19.

CARL was always jumping out on top of me from behind
hedges on College Road & Magazine Road even on Western
Road, creeping low in his black raincoat on Jury's bridge
making me leap for the sky, like. He loved giving me frights,
Only a bit of blackguarding! Dora said that was a sign. Of what
she wasn't sure. Then he said he was coming to see
my record collection & I took a box to St. Vincent De
Paul's before he came round with Tom. They said they
wanted to *view Palace Place View.* Carole King, Janis Ian
Cat Stevens, Bob Dylan & Don McClean, I was packing them
all in, wondering why I didn't have *Joy Division*
when I loved Ian Curtis so much. I was singing *Love Will
Tear Us Apart* & nearly crying when I packed *The Pretenders*
by mistake. Nearly forgot the worst—*The Best of The Stylistics.*

20.

DISCO was only an embarrassment. The thought of Tom looking
over his glasses at the Stylistics made me sick. *Calm down,* said
Dora & I said that Best said that Ian Curtis died to bring us the
music like & Dora said, *Well, I never heard of him* & I said,
Sure he hung himself on a clotheshorse! & Dora said *That's impossible*
& I said, *Oh God, maybe I am wrong!* But Dora stood by
the counter in Curtin's Bar, taking her music advice from
Pierce Curtin, taping Billy Holiday & Nina Simone.
Music was fierce scary—Carl rattling in his raincoat, *What?*
You fucking like THEM? Tom standing there, silently fingering his
blue button-down shirt. He'd no time for Bob Dylan either
& I was so busy covering my tracks, that by the time they came
round to see us, I'd no records at all
& they weren't sure what to make of that.

SMOKEY, Myra Curtin's cat sat on a stool & Pierce
played Billie Holiday who sounded like a cat. That was
a compliment to Billie from me even though *cat* was
an insult in Cork. Dora got mad with Carl when he said
the chips in Mandys were *fucking cat.* She said cats were victims
of Sectarianism only she wouldn't say if protestants were
dogs or cats when Tom asked because that was only more of it.
Smokey had chocolate-coloured tears in his eyes & on his blue
-grey cheeks, a spotted red bow around his neck. He looked French.
Myra said, *Don't ask me a word about that cat & his dark tears
because it breaks my heart,* Myra's eyes were on Pierce polishing
the same pint glass with a black & cream Guinness tea towel,
looking up as if his own words floated on the ceiling.
Dora wrote them all down in a pale green Aisling copybook
with a round tower & a flock of swallows on the front.

22.

IT'S easy to impress the young eedjits, Myra said. No one
listened to her except me because I didn't know how
to get away. Pierce & Myra'd been young anarchists,
nearly thrown out of Cork only that Myra's father was a Super.
But now their hair was *turning grey,* Myra said, making
Pierce look in the mirror. & he was still looking at it now
tossing his dark locks with the grey bits, like a pony
as Dora wrote notes under him. With a pink face. Myra said royal
blue was a very hard colour to wear, looking at Dora's batwing sleeves.
He's telling her to read Bury My Heart at Wounded Knee.
I know by the gatche of him, said Myra. *I bet you anything*
that's what she's written in the copybook, Bury My Heart
At Wounded Knee, that's the sorry hook he draws them in on.
I looked in the Aisling copybook & Myra was right.

23.

EVERYONE has their dreams like, Dora defended Pierce. *Okay so!*
I said & I went into Matthews pretending I was buying supplies
for very important work. Raw Umber, Grenadine, Sap
Green, Lamp Black. The special pens for calligraphy, pastel
crayons, soft blue, pink, the cream cartridge paper I would
never use. My careful diagrams with all the colours –
Good diagrams don't mean you're Leonardo, said Justin when Clodagh
showed him my copybook. *Pure Useless,* he said about me now.
I should have bought geometry sets & set squares but I bought
a packet of children's colouring pencils with a picture of Noah
& the Ark on the front of the box. I wished I could be
drawing all the animals two-by two instead of cutting them up
& then I went into *May's* sweetshop behind the courthouse
on Sheare's Street – it smelt like the inside of an Easter egg.

24.

MAY was fierce pink, blushing under her white beehive, shovelling
Chocolate Ices with a silver shovel into a white paper
bag. Her fingernails were mauve & she had a three-piece purple
& lilac trouser suit inside her white coat. *It's only sometimes
the Traveller has them.* She didn't know why they were called
Ices but they came from Germany. Their tiny, pleated foil cases were
red, blue & green. Once she had chocolate Volkswagens.
But never again so I bought three bags of Ices in case
the Traveller didn't have them next time. I felt like throwing
myself down under the Number 8 bus but not really.
& then Donny Lane appeared at the end of Sheare's Street
in his khaki jacket, big blue glasses, flicking his long
red hair. He needed Dora & me for a Séance – his
parents were killed in a crash & he was dying to reach them.

25.

ON Wilton Road, I looked at my wristwatch, four o'clock.
The Blue Arsenic hour, Dora called it. I often heard
Justin's voice at that hour. Nagging like mad. & four in
the morning wasn't too good either, only I wasn't
always awake. Oh I'd never pass my exams. My nerves.
Justin said I should give up. *Will you even get into nursing now*
anyway? No self-respecting hospital matron would give the time of
day to a girl with muck all over her eyes. Better girls than you have
had to rely on pull & it's the boat to England for the rest of the scum.
I asked Donny, *if I can't face the dogfish, how can I do nursing?*
& Donny said, *Nature red in tooth & claw!* I said, *How*
d'you mean? – sure he was saying something important. But he
put his hand to his forehead, knocking his glasses, *I have*
no ambition! he said. He was only talking about himself.

26.

WE came to the back door of Donny's house, Carl
was inside already, sitting at the table, cutting out
the letters under the light of a pink plastic lamp which
belonged to Donny's mother. *What's your excuse for this
invasion!* Donny roared. *Sure you told me about the key under
the stone like!* Donny wasn't admiring Carl but I was. His
stone-blue mod trousers tapered to the ankle over Oxblood
Docs with a Band-Aid over the right toe. Carl said Donny
promised him a blood-red steak if he came out & I said
he'd promised me a steak too which would be a break
from the 149 packets of Erin soup at the flat, mostly
Minestrone which Clodagh put into my rucksack on Sunday
nights saying she was worried that the studying was bad
for my nerves. *Promise me you'll think seriously about nursing?*

27.

BEST & Tom pounded at the back door with a fella called Murphy.
He'd red tips on the spikes of his hair, a luminous cobalt-
blue vest & no coat in the fierce wind. As they burst in the door
he raised his toolbox like a flag. *I bet they've heard about the steaks
in your deep freezer, Donny!* said Carl, licking his lips.
Jesus, it's a séance not steaks we're having! said Donny
Can ye not think of something else apart from yeer stomachs?
& Dora said, *Now! Donny's mind is on higher things!*
I said I wanted to be a vegetarian! & *sure who's stopping you?*
said Murphy. The bare windows were pitch & the bench I was
sitting on gave a hop when Murphy sat down beside me.
He asked me if I'd ever heard of Beelzebubba &
I looked at him & he said *Calm down, girl, it's only a record—
have you never listened to The Dead Milkmen?*

28.

YOU don't know The Dead Milkmen? A girl like you! "My Many
Smells"? "Punk Rock Girls, like?" I looked down in shame. The years wasted
on Janis Ian, Cat Stevens, Bob Dylan but I said I loved
Ian Curtis. *He died for us!* I meant to say he died for the
music but Murphy bowed his head anyway. *He did, girl!*
Did I know Camus? I only knew his name. Murphy said
Camus was an Existentialist. I asked if it had
anything to do with Utilitarianism
because Dora was one. Murphy said it had fuck all to
do with it. *God, I know nothing!* I said. *Knowledge is power,
girl!* Murphy gave me a slug of his cider before he
threw the flagon of Bulmers up on his head & Carl said
women with power could be dangerous. *Only
blackguarding!* he said when Dora showed him her American Eagle face.

29.

MURPHY wore leather bondage trousers under his blue vest.
I hated muscles but I liked Murphy's & his long donkey
face. *Camus,* Murphy said & Carl said, *Albert.* & Murphy said,
That's right, Albert Camus. Albert believed in absurdity,
that's the difference between what you feel & what the world
really is. & I said, *It's like Science Practicals!* Murphy
drank again, cords stuck out on his neck like reins &
said *If Science is that cat, you shouldn't lower yourself*
worrying about it! Dora said, *Don't say cat* & Murphy
said *Okay!* & put his hands in the air as if Dora
had a gun, *Human beings are absurd because they look*
for meanings in things that have no fucking meaning at all.
Carl's eyes were red with sparks. He said no way were things that
simple & I should stop gulping cider, it didn't suit me, like.

30.

DONNY stood up & shouted *Ciúineas* & Murphy asked if
Donny was the teacher. *He's a demonstrator,* I said.
*Jesus Christ Almighty, I am just trying to have a fucking
séance in peace, if you don't want to, there's the door!*
& Best said, *But when are you serving the red steaks?*
Donny asked Best did he think he was a pure fool
altogether & Best stood up, *Sure the band are here now,
it's too fucking late. Stuff your steaks, you bourgeois Physics
Demonstrator.* Tom said over his glasses, *Are you trying
to pretend you're working class now?* but Best wasn't
listening, his ear cocked to the clucking of the chicken
squawks coming from the black shadows running
around the front garden. Donny stood up too, throwing
his long red hair over the epaulettes of his army jacket,
roaring like a lion, *Did you give those knackers my address?*

31.

MANSLAUGHTER's old Morris Minor was parked at the gate,
a rusting bug under the orange street lamps. *Scumbags!* said Donny
but he drew back when he saw the band springing through the high
grass with their cans of shaving foam, Jimmy Barry waving a hatchet
in front. *Is it real?* yowled Donny. *Jimmy's the bass player,* said Carl
& isn't Best very forgiving after Jimmy poured petrol
into his two blue eyes? Tom got his donkey jacket, *That's the*
end of my steak so sure, he said as he followed Best &
Donny said that Tom could write that down. Best mock-boxed &
karate-chopped outside with Jimmy. Their shadows were reeling,
sparks flying from the steel caps of their boots as they kicked.
Are they friends now? I asked & Carl said he supposed they were.
Donny said that true friends were hard to find & that we were not
to give those notice boxes the soot of looking at them.

32.

I'D pins & needles in my hand. We propped our right arms up
with the left ones but the letters never moved. When Donny groaned
Come on lads, for feck's sake concentrate! the back door creaked &
a black dog pushed in with one pearl-blue eye, nails clittering
on the tiles. We kept our hands over the glass as we looked over our
shoulders at him, rummaging in the dustbin for scraps. *He
often comes during a séance,* said Donny. Dora shuddered inside
her long blue dress. *Sure that dog is only after the steaks,* said Murphy
winking at Dora. *Like every other fecker out tonight!* said Donny.
Murphy said he wouldn't touch the steaks if you boiled him in oil
because he was a vegetarian. *Do you remember that night you were
concentrating so hard on the glass that you didn't notice
Finny the Hat coming in, frying up one of your own steaks & offering
it to you?* said Murphy. *I don't want to remember it,* said Donny.

33.

YE'RE just not taking it serious, said Donny, licking his hand.
Carl asked what was he doing & Donny said he was checking
for salt. *Is that a sign?* I asked & Donny roared *Ciúineas!* again.
Dora held her stomach, still looking like an American Eagle.
Carl stood up to ease his waistband, his Mod blue trousers were
tight, like something a bullfighter would wear. The dog found
a butter wrapper in the bin, started licking it across the tiles.
Ciúineas! said Murphy & winked at me. *Why didn't you go with
the band?* asked Carl & Murphy said that he thought that Carl &
himself were supposed to be doing Wrecky afterwards. Carl
straightened his shoulders, looked into the big black rectangle
of Donny's kitchen window & said, *Fucking Brilliant Altogether!*
Murphy said, *Sure we'll bring Herself too*! & I nearly burst with
excitement, I didn't know what Wrecky was but I was wanted.

34.

OH she's a proper punkette all right, boy, said Murphy with
his manly rippling muscles. His toolbox swept past Donny's
strawberry blonde head bowed sadly over the dog. I felt guilty,
a bad apostle leaving Gethsemane. We chinked our cider
bottles down the road, Carl & Murphy's faces were yellow
in the orange light & I supposed mine must be the same.
When I drained the last slug out of my Bulmers & put it down
by the kerb, Murphy said, *Oh God hang on to that bottle,
girl!* He shouted *Beelzebubba* & jumped on the red crispy leaves
as Carl caught hold of my hand. He had to prove himself
because of his father, he said. A wind cut in suddenly &
I pulled up the zip of my wet-look anorak. I heard Justin saying
Show me your company! I couldn't bear it so I said to Murphy
Jesus I'd love some Pondies now! & he said I was a hard woman.

35.

IT was hard explaining to Dora because she didn't
understand about punk & anarchy & the feeling
I had when Murphy stood beside me in the middle of
the Clashduv Estate singing, *I Want You To Want Me*,
my cold ears ticking like clocks. The three of us took fierce aim.
Carl stepped back & made a fantastic sound in the back of
his throat but he missed his window. I threw my brick in the
air & hit myself on the head. We ran up the road, screaming
Power to the Under Classes & *Up Your Arse!* A man threw
open a sash window & roared, *Thundering blackguards!*
Carl pulled my arm hard & told me to run before we were
seen. I felt like Billy the Kid galloping away. *I'm after ringing the
Bridewell!* said the man & we ran for miles, my breath tasted
sweet & sparkling, like red Tanora coming out of a bottle.

36.

DID you even know where you were? said Dora when I said Murphy
took us to a wild bit of the city. *It was another planet,* I said.
Torn by briars, up on top of giant cliffs of grass looking down
on the yellow necklaces of the city lights, waiting
for Murphy to start laughing at me for hitting myself with
my own brick but he said I was the biggest Absurdist,
that it was the greatest existentialist statement
he'd ever seen enacted in Cork City. Then Carl brought me
underneath a leafless tree & started kissing me so Murphy
had to go away. I was fierce sad afterwards but Dora said
that was the cider talking. *Thank God you got rid of that fella,*
she said. Carl will be all right if ye ever get into trouble
because of his father but if you're caught with Murphy you'll
never be able to go home again. I wondered what that would be like.

37.

DORA said she couldn't believe it out of me. Wrecking
innocent people's houses. *A Vandal! What's that about?*
I couldn't say. We were in Curtin's drinking Stag & Dora
walked into the Ladies as a protest when she saw
Carl coming in with Best. She ran freezing water over
her blue hands, soaping & soaping. *I've had enough of those
boyos!* She said the spitting was pure disgusting & looked at
me as if I was doing it & I said I thought it
was fierce disgusting too but it was Punk. Dora asked me if
I had a mind of my own & I said I fucking had.
Then Myra opened the door & said *Isn't the black lovely
on you, Imelda! Make the best of it while you can.
A woman should never wear black between the age of forty
& sixty.* When Myra went out, Dora said, *Have I gone red?*

38.

DORA was reading *Bury My Heart At Wounded Knee*
& I was going everywhere with Carl, we were going out.
I was fierce proud of his shaved head, stone-blue Mod Trousers &
the Elastoplast covering the hole on his Oxblood Docs.
After two weeks we were sitting in Wilton shopping centre
eating custard slices for a hangover when he asked me to
marry him & I said *Yes! I will!* He wanted five children
although I wasn't so sure about that because someone said
I was too highly strung for children. *Take no notice of Justin!*
He said our own family would be *just brilliant* but not yet
although getting contraceptives was *An Ordeal.* Having to go into
the Family Planning Clinic with the whole of Cork staring.
He said he *felt hunted* & I felt guilty. More than anything
I wanted him to feel Manly.

39.

IF Carl didn't feel Manly, he was a wasp. Dora said
you were safe ten days before & ten days after your
period but when I checked again, she went red & said
she wasn't sure & then she said she'd asked the three Arts girls
living in Glasheen Road & they all said it was true, like
but who were the three Arts girls? I wanted to know. Then
Dora said maybe it was better that we asked the experts if
we could go into the Family Planning Clinic in Tuckey Street only
we were afraid we might be seen. Carl ran in & out very
fast himself with his Madness hat pulled down over his
eyes & the brown paper bag hidden in the pocket of
his donkey jacket. Getting them was only the start of
the problem, he said & *you're telling me*, I said & he said
what do you mean? & I said, *Sure, I'm only agreeing with you!*

40.

MY nerves were electric. What was I going to do
about them? Someone said every student who'd taken
Botany, Zoology, Physics & Chemistry
was going to fail whether they liked it or not because
they knew full well they should be doing Maths. The Physics
Department wasn't going to let them get away with
that blackguarding even though the system had allowed
fifteen red-handed Maths-dodgers including myself to
choose that *lazy combination*. I heard this from someone else
because I wasn't at the lecture. The failure rate for
First Physics was 70% Professor Mahony
told us the first day. I thought I should warn Justin of the
pit at my feet. *Now you tell me!* he said. *Trust you to be
one of the fifteen. Oh Round up the usual Suspects!*

41.

USELESS! Useless! said Justin, his disembodied voice was
always prodding me, the nervous cow. Even when I was in
in a Physics practical. We had black leads & red leads & a board
with a light bulb. If we attached the leads the right way the bulb
lit up. The first fellow did it & then all the bulbs followed, every
lit bulb with an excited face over it. A fierce wind ran
through me. I plugged & unplugged faster & faster.
The first fellow said it was like chess, after three moves
there was 121 million possible outcomes. *Just think of it!* he said.
As if I could, plugging & unplugging, my stubborn bulb dark
as Beelzebub. The demonstrator who looked like Bobby
Sands had to take it away. *Have I failed?* I asked & he said
it was not for him to say. When I looked down from the high
blue glass box of the Science building, it felt like I was falling.

42.

FEBRUARY was bitter & our money was running out.
Dora didn't want to go to Curtin's even with all the free
drink we got from sentimental ex-students of U.C.C.
& a bottle of Stag for this lovely girl! But we went for one of
Myra's toasted sandwiches. They weren't toasted just melted
in the microwave. The bread went soft & white instead of brown
& crisp & the cheese ran out at the sides, orange rivers
on the worn willow pattern plates. Myra told us not to
touch them until they were *coagulated*. Dora gave me a look.
& Myra caught her looking, whirled around in her baby blue
bat-wing sleeved jumper & said that it was convenient
for people to think she was mad but that she read books too.
What about Jean Rhys? Dora said she'd heard of her. *But
are you learning her lessons though?* asked Myra.

43·

MYRA said Jean Rhys wrote a book called *Wide Sargasso Sea*
about Mr Rochester's first wife, the one they all thought was mad.
He'd her locked up so he could get on with his womanizing.
I was afraid to look at Myra or Dora. I wished
Pierce would come back from wherever he was. I stroked Smokey
under his crimson collar & his purrs crescendoed.
I opened my pocket-sized packet of Kleenex & wiped
his brown tears. Myra said Smokey'd have to take the long walk
soon & I said *No!* & Myra said that it was a desperate
responsibility to have the power of life & death
over another creature, *Own an animal, ultimately
you're the executioner!* Two pale faces peered out of
the Bushmills mirror behind Myra.
I looked down at the beer-stained ground. *She's mad,* I said
after but Dora said she agreed with Myra 100%.

44.

I THOUGHT Dora was out with me although she said
she wasn't. She was reading fairy tales & when
the boys said she was childish, she said it was a
Feminist Issue & I agreed. *I've always loved Cinderella's
blue & pink dresses in the Ladybird books!* I said in The Long
Valley & everyone looked away in embarrassment.
It's the colours! I said but still they looked away from me.
Murphy said that he heard that Dora was in favour
of abortion & I said that she was not, she was in
favour of *choice* & that I was, too, because the world
was overpopulated & didn't people put down cats
out of kindness? I thought Dora would be pleased
when I stood up for her but her face was turned away too,
she looked like she wanted to be sick.

45.

MURPHY said he'd seen a fair number of kittens drowned
& kindness didn't come into it but he'd seen the women
throwing condoms around Patrick Street & he was *out-&-out*
in favour of that because *College girls don't know much
about biology.* I said that Dora was Utilitarian. I thought
maybe she'd like that better but she only shivered & pulled
her steel-blue coat & said she was sick of the cold &
that the tip of my nose was pure pink. I got up to go
to the Ladies (to have a look at my nose) & Murphy said
Utilitarianism was the *Gear Knock*. He asked her had she
ever met Mick the Commie & Dora said,
*For fuck's sake, as if all the people who are something
should know each other!* Carl said he saw her looking up books
in the library after & looking desperate worried.

46.

DORA said Pierce came back to our flat on College Road
the night I was out in Clashduv doing Wrecky. I asked
in what way had he come back to the flat but she went red
& said, *Let's move on from that, it's a matter of urgency
here.* She hadn't asked the girls in Glasheen about the safe
time at all. It was Pierce who'd told her & he was wrong. The
big eedjit didn't know because Myra couldn't have
children. Dora had gone into Easons on Patrick Street
to read up on the subject standing up in a corner because
she hadn't had a period for sixty days & at that,
an icy-blue plume poured into my stomach. *What are you
going to do?* I asked. But what was *I* going to do?
How could I even pray to God when he (or she) was as
unreal as the three Arts girls living on the Glasheen Road?

47.

WE were standing in the wind on Western Road when
Donny Kane appeared in a rusty duffle coat & said
we could come to a séance as long as we didn't bring the boys.
The black dog was there, pawing the dustbin with his
clittery yellow nails, looking back at us with his one
milk-blue eye, red tongue out a mile. I loved dogs but I just
wasn't sure about him. Donny opened a tin of Batchelor's
Beans. He'd made a new set of letters with a red magic marker.
Bubble writing. *Bloody fecking nothing, Jesus!* said Donny
after a while, sitting back in his chair but we kept at it,
pins and needles in our fingers, listening to lonely cars
turning around in the estate, footsteps, the rattle of a baby
buggy. The dog's jaws kept clicking, he slurped every bean
in the bowl, his yawn was desperate high-pitched. It hurt my ears.

48.

HE'S still hungry. Donny opened the deep freeze, fried up four
steaks, said we might as well *eat like a family. I wouldn't be
surprised if that dog pulled a chair up to the table & ate
his with a knife and fork,* said Dora after telling Donny
he should tie back his hair when he was cooking. I couldn't
eat after she said that. The dog ate the most of all the
dinners. *The poor fecker,* said Donny. *He should be put down
if he has no home. It's not fair on him.* The dog stopped
eating, turned round, sat up on his haunches. Donny said
he was reminded of the Russian dog Laika who went
into space. *Oh God, his blue eye!* I said when we walked home
& Dora got into my bed because our hands were violet
with the cold. I had to drink nearly two thirds of a bottle
of Benylin to close that one dog's eye in the dark.

49.

CARL said Bobby Sands was a murderer & I got mad.
I had my own Troubles. I didn't want to think of them
starving themselves into their coffins & Murph said hunger
striking was suicide the same as Ian Curtis.
Will you stop talking about Life & Death, I said & Murph
said, *Isn't Dora a Utilitarian?* & I said,
My grandfather fought for the freedom of this country! &
burst out of The Long Valley. Carl came after me & said
only eedjits went on about the IRA & they were
pure cat with their flares & long hair & I fell in Winthrop
Street & cut my lip & he still said I was an eedjit. I saw the
blue light of an ambulance coming for me. Only it wasn't.
I walked down Washington Street, licking my salty blood.
Carl sang *Love Will Tear Us Apart*, it always cheered him up.

50.

IT was our first row. It hammered on all night until Dora
said her head was opening. Carl wanted to know why I spent
so much time talking to John McVeigh in The Teach Beag.
Drawing attention to yourself! I always stood by John's
elbow so I could hear him order *A Guinness & Raspberry*
in his Belfast accent. He had long black hair nearly to
his waist & black shorter wings at either side which he flicked.
He always played *A Whiter Shade of Pale* on the juke box.
His whole family had been burnt out & he was on the
run from the Brits. *But he's had so much tragedy like & he's
on the run from the Brits*, I said & Carl said no one who was
really on the run from the Brits would be talking about
it in pubs to eedjits. Carl said his father said *that type
are only after money. But sure I have none!* I said.

51.

DORA's sister gave her money because *It would kill Mammy*.
Pro-Life people stopped people on the boat to England &
Dora didn't know if the Guards did it too. Wasn't it
illegal? We didn't know. Was it Murder? We didn't
know if we'd be stopped on the train to Dublin. We wanted
to have tests faraway so no one would know. Snowflakes
began to fall on the glass roof as we stood on the black
& white tiles of Kent station. Dora's desert boots were dyed
velvety blue, the laces were navy. She tucked them under
her shivering powder-blue skirt. We felt fierce sick.
Wrecky on the Clashduv estate was nothing compared
to this. We couldn't say the things we were thinking.
By the time the burnt-orange & black train was ready to
board, the pale green ticket was damp in my hand.

52.

I DON'T know why Dora brought a suitcase of books with her.
She said she felt sick again. I was feeling sick too. The night before
in The Teach Beag Murphy had been talking about the Price
sisters being force-fed, everyone kept talking about hunger-
striking & Dora said she dreamt that her big sister &
mother served her plates of shit & forced her to eat it with
a knife & fork. She told me this as we were stepping down
at the train station. *Jesus Christ,* I said & Dora said,
Go into the toilet & stick your fingers down your throat.
Afterwards it felt like how a Good Confession used to feel – fierce light..
As I was getting on the bus, the conductor said,
You'd see better without the sunglasses so I took them off.
Snow had stopped most of the buses like there really was a
God who might send a shower of locusts after us.

53.

DORA said she brought the suitcase because she was tempted
to go straight to the North Wall, get the ferry to England
& put an end to it. *What about me?* I said. Dora said
I was free to come too. We walked from Trinity College
to Merrion Square in drifts after the buses stopped, passing
through Nassau Street which I'd never seen before outside
of the Monopoly board. Donny had loaned me his duffle
coat but Dora's powder-blue cotton skirt was soaked to the
waist. I'd boiled my jeans in a big saucepan of Black Dylon
the Sunday before & the black dye ran in the snow, followed
us in grey streaks. The woman gave us the results & said
Don't be rushed. She hoped we'd people we could talk to. *Yes,
we have,* we said. On the train back, I thought there were four of
us sitting on two seats. *Do you hear that clock?* asked Dora.

54.

WE took out the vintage clothes we'd bought in Jenny Vander's
on George's Street. Our excuse if we were questioned about
our journey. *You don't know who is watching you!* said Dora.
I had a 50s petrol-blue Shantung three quarter-length
coat with big buttons. After sliding the wide-skirted
polka-dotted dresses up and down the rack a few times,
Dora'd said she couldn't try anything on, it was too cold.
She bought a turtle brooch but she dropped it on the train &
a man stood on it. The fake pearl of the turtle's body fell out
& Dora held the empty frame of brooch to her dark
blue eye. Just like the black dog, a bad sign even though she
insisted that there was no such thing. We never used a code
word. It felt wrong to call them names like that. But what we could
call them, we didn't know.

55.

THERE was only the two (or four) of us. Carl thought it was
better that he stay away from me. His father was getting fierce
strict & examining the size of his pupils. He had heard that
Carl was *mixing up & down with* a *dolly-bird*. & I asked
Why didn't you say that I'm a punkette? Carl said he was afraid
of his father cutting him off but he would definitely
get me the three hundred pounds, *I've done the research.*
I wondered if this was one of our five future children?
No one asked me what I wanted & I was really hoping
they would. Pierce was consoling Myra & digging the grave
for Smokey. Dora said he'd no choice, it was her he was
thinking of because Myra said she would tell Dora's mother
& it would kill her. Dora's mother had always said that
It's the grandmother who suffers most in these cases.

56.

MURPHY was in training for football so he drank a Rock
Shandy, dancing in front of the juke box in The Teach Beag.
His violent royal blue vest was strapped in with scarlet braces.
He said he was thinking of getting a vasectomy.
I looked at Dora & she looked at both of us with her
American Eagle face as if I had something to do
with it & I didn't even know what a vasectomy
was. He said that he'd be frightened to have anything to
do with a college girl. *And have they asked you?* said Dora.
I felt that wasn't fair but Murph struck back like a rattle snake.
I'm not the one who's wearing a big Holy Mary blue smock,
& I said *Shut Up!* Murphy shook his head, *Don't know what ye're*
learning up there? It's not biology anyway that's for sure!
I went into the toilet & made myself sick.

57.

BE careful, said Dora. *Remember how the Price Sisters got
anorexia.* & I said, *I'm not in prison.* & Dora said *there's
more than one way of force-feeding.* Murphy slurped his bright
orange *Rock Shandy* right under Dora's eagle nose & said,
So how's the Utilitarianism going anyway?
I'm ignoring you, boy! said Dora. Best came in with Jimmy
Barry & Jimmy Barry winked at me, *How's the culchie?* Murphy
said, *Stop the prejudice.* It was an awful evening even
before Noreen Campbell arrived, wearing a wine beret, pulled
exaggeratingly to one side. She said she knew
& supposed I was going to England. I said yes, wondering
when I'd actually made up my mind. I whispered to Dora
that it was a fright to God that Noreen knew & Dora
said it was a fright to God that Noreen existed.

58.

*HOW can you read Wide Sargasso Sea after Myra attacking
me?* attacked Dora. *Sure I wouldn't have known about it
otherwise!* I said. I read it to myself when she wasn't
around, bouncing my voice against the dirty sky-blue walls
of the flat. I thundered about justice, reading aloud,
'It's a cold word. I tried it out,' she said speaking in a low voice.
I stamped my foot, said it was a damn cold word & a lie, like
& thought about Mammy who threw all her clothes in the river
because she didn't want any more children. & then she died.
Justice only reminded me of Justin & he wasn't just,
he was judgemental. He showed me how disgusting I was.
I was afraid Dora would rear up on me but I wanted to say
that there was no justice when Pierce was the one who'd got
two of us in trouble with the wrong information.

59.

THERE was a bottle of Dubonnet in the kitchen cupboard
I threw it back & followed with some Benylin. It was savage
cold. *Would the landlord miss the collapsing chair if we broke
it up for firewood?* I asked Dora. We hadn't had a fire
since the time Tom was caught stealing a bale of briquettes
outside a house on Blarney Street. Dora was like a briar.
The cold is the least of our problems, she kicked the collapsing
chair. She said she felt like killing someone. Carl had told Best & Tom
about London & now they were coming too. For the craic. *As if
they don't know,* said Dora. *& how come everyone knows anyway?
Sure we couldn't just disappear,* said Carl. *That's a red flag.* He
rubbed my cold hands & told me he loved me. I forced myself
to look into his eyes, *I love you too,* I said & vomited Dubonnet
over his boots.

60.

CARL & Pierce paid for a double berth & Dora & I
lay in it. *We've made our bed & we now must lie on it,*
I said & Dora looked at me. Carl was on deck with Best.
He'd got a part-time job in The Western Star. *A Cess Pit
for Dropouts,* Justin called it when we drove past my first night
in College. I got a small loan from the AIB bank.
The man in the bank said *Brains & beauty!* He'd never met
a girl studying Physics before. It was clear to him, he
said I wouldn't be long in the red. *You must be very brainy.*
Jean Rhys was right, there was no justice, people got praised for
all the wrong things. I was touched that Carl got the job. Dora
said she wasn't touched by any of it, she was going
celibate. We stood on the deck, the ship cut a white V
through the black waves. I vomited over the side.

61.

MY appointment was for Monday & Dora's was for the
Tuesday. Sunday we went to Dingwalls on Camden Lock.
It's the longest bar in London, said Carl. He was the expert.
He'd been to London the summer of 80, saw all the
great bands, stood next to The Bodysnatchers in a club &
asked Joe Jackson for a light. We had to go down an alley
behind the market, a shack with a red door, like a place
out of a dream & then out of nowhere Murphy appeared to us,
his red head newly dyed. *Where did you come from?* said Carl.
I could ask you the same question! said Murphy. He was over
for his first cousin's wedding in Hackney Town Hall.
The house next door to her squat had a blue plaque to Burlington
Bertie. Murphy danced sideways with an invisible cane.
Carl whispered that Murphy was only following us around.
Everywhere I go! Dora threw her cigarette on the ground.

62.

SOMEONE had blues. Ten Pole Tudor came on, we rushed out
onto the floor, demented for the last hurrah. Shouting
the words of 'The Swords of a Thousand Men' – *deep in the castle
back from the wars, back with my baby. Hoorah! Hoorah!*
Dora refused to dance, stood stubborn, smoking Gitanes as the
rest of us pogoed & sweated & took off our jumpers.
I nearly fell in the struggle, my second-hand real sailor
jacket from the Coal Quay was so tight. Carl said, *Delroy
T. Johnson,* reading the name tag on the jacket. *And where
is Delroy now?* he asked looking philosophical &
I felt fierce sad. Carl & myself had sex all night because
Carl said we might as well take advantage. I felt desperate
afterwards & no matter how hard I tried to think it didn't
matter, it did. It was never the same again.

63.

WE only had the address, Carl got the name of the clinic
from some girl who didn't want to be brought into it.
I asked if it was different from the one at the back of
Cosmopolitan & Carl said *Sure they're blacked out
in the Irish Cosmopolitans!* Well, I'd never looked,
had I? Carl was under *Massive Strain* & I had an alias.
What next? said Dora but Carl said it was a great idea.
My name is Jackie Clarke! I said as we left the bed &
breakfast & then I had to sit down on the stone steps
of a four-story house in Pentonville to put my head
between my knees. I asked Carl if he thought it was right.
Is it really like? I said & he said we'd paid now. We went down
into the underground at Holloway & the noise of the Tube
went through my stomach as if I'd swallowed the tracks.

64.

AT King's Cross, I looked down the steps of the escalator
moving like a long elongated mouth & I was afraid
to put my foot on it. I didn't think I could, didn't want to
be carried down so deep. A man in a bowler hat barked
Move! Carl put his hand on my back & told the man he had
no manners. I stepped on sideways looking at a poster for
The Mousetrap because if I looked down, I knew I would fall.
The tube map comforted me in the carriage, sky-blue for the
Victoria line, I said to myself & then I wanted to stay underground.
I was like a mole prised from a burrow when Carl said *Next
stop Brixton.* I followed Carl, following the A-Z to the tall
redbrick. In Cork the *Red Brick* was the madhouse where Justin
was sure he'd be driven by my carry on. A man in a suit
came out with a sobbing blonde woman. I stopped walking.

65.

YOU'RE *doing brilliant,* said Carl. *I don't think so,* I said
looking at the woman who seemed way too old for this.
We're here now, he said & I moved again, no longer a small
mole but a giant stumbling cow. Then I was in a prefab
& it was like Benetton's, all the girls were tanned & very
good-looking. Their pink & orange & blue sweaters had
fuzzy haloes from the morning sun coming through
the windows. They were quiet, turning the pages of Women's
Realm, Woman Own, Cosmopolitan but I heard two of them
speaking Spanish. They seemed Worldly Wise. I wondered
what Murphy meant when he asked Dora, *Is reproduction
the cheapest method of recruiting moral agents?* &
Dora said, *You don't know what you're talking about boy!* But
I liked Murphy asking questions. & then when I looked
around for Carl he was gone.

66.

JACKIE Clarke! shouted a tall English sister with red cheeks.
Her dark blue uniform was clipped at the waist & there was
a white frilled pillbox on her head like a crown. *Little Irish*!
she said when she heard my Cork accent. The examining
doctor said I was twelve weeks & I said I thought I was eight
but that only seemed to madden her. Sister came back in
& told the doctor she was taking me away from *The Foreigners.*
Next patient, please! said the doctor. Sister said
it was a pity my boyfriend had gone because he could
have stayed. Her chest was staked with badges & the upside
down silver watch which she watched as she pumped up the
sphygmomanometer. I went off on the trolley in a pink gown
& a surgeon passed with gloved hands in the air. I was afraid
to tell them I thought the trolley was going too fast.

67.

I WOKE screaming & struggling, asking them to leave me alone.
They had something inside of me. *Tranquilo! Tranquilo!*
said the Spanish girls, upset for me. I wanted them to stay but
Sister drove them away, *Leave that girl alone!* she said.
She poured a glass of water to wash down two small
yellow circles of Valium. I slept for a while & then
she woke me. Carl was on the phone from the pub
where the wedding crowd went after Hackney Town Hall
Murphy's cousin really was getting married & she was
wearing the Cork colours, red and white. *The Blood and Bandage,*
Carl said. He sounded drunk. I stood on the blue tiles of the
cold hallway & wondered who owned the yellow dressing gown
I was wearing. *Ghost Town* was playing at the other end.
I could hear myself crying like an echo down the line.

68.

CARL said the lads couldn't believe that Linton Kwesi
Johnson drove our taxi to the clinic & when I said I
couldn't believe it either he got angry & said *It's the drugs –
those bastards have tampered with your mind!* I told him that
the Valium was pure useless & that I wasn't upset myself
only there was another person inside in me protesting. I
heard Carl say, *They're after splitting her personality* before
he passed the phone to Dora & then they realised she was
the wrong person. I could hear Tom saying, *Ah Jesus, no.
Look at her face.* So I ended up crying to the bride who was real
because Murphy never lied. It was a real wedding with a real
bride who said she didn't care if I had a split personality.
I apologised for bursting into her wedding & when I asked
about Dora, she said not to worry, *Sure Dora's flying, girl!*

69.

WHEN I came out I couldn't remember if it was
morning or evening. I was with everyone except Dora.
& I was laughing like mad. We went down two flights
into Wards Irish House in Piccadilly. I wanted
to be underground. I wanted to stand on the tube platform
& feel the fierce wind. Wards had pale green & white tiles because –
Tom said – it had been an Edwardian lavatory.
The counter was silvery metal & they had draught Guinness.
I had to sit on a barrel digging into me & I believed
it was pure Justice. Carl bought me a pint & we took Blues again
only I didn't go up, I went down like & vomited
three times. Carl said it was a pity we didn't have a
camera for a photograph of ourselves in front of the statue
of Eros & Tom said, *She's probably had enough of Eros now.*

70.

I'D caused enough trouble & I was fierce thirsty. A Belfast
barman with blue chin said I was a cheapskate when
I ordered more soda water. He didn't believe me when
I said I didn't know it was free, we paid for it at home.
Do you mean the South? He was just like Justin banging a bottle
of Schweppes on the bar counter with a cross face.
Tom butted in & said over his glasses we were from
The Republic & called him *A Fucking Orange Bastard*
under his breath. I switched to Coke. *You've your
work cut out for you trying to persuade anyone over here
you're British,* Tom said to the barman afterwards.
We're all Paddies now! & it was true. Everywhere we
went for the next two days, that's what we were &
it was a relief & a disguise like wearing a uniform.

71.

WE couldn't afford berths on the way back so we sat up
all night in the bar & the table was so sticky the
glasses kept sticking to it & two old Paddies shared
all their Bushmills with us. Our accents made them sentimental.
I was afraid that wasn't fair but everyone just kept singing
I'm a rambler, I'm a gambler & a long way from home.
Best moved to a different seat from us, reading *1984*.
& when Dora asked him, *Why now?* He said, *Because it's 1981!*
He was never the same again either, starting hanging
out with his engineering class & drinking with them
in the college bar after his job interviews, looking
clean with his new buzz cut in the middle of the
rest of them with their long hair. *Country cunts,* said
Jimmy Barry, but I didn't mind. I hated the engineers too.

72.

BEST sat in the College bar with the engineers every day
bawling, *We are the engineers, we are the best, we are the
engineers & fuck all the rest. & Fuck Best too*, said Dora
to me. We were trying but it was hard to talk to each other.
Once we both rushed to get sick in the toilet of The Long
Valley at the same time & I said, *You first.* Afterwards
she said, *Why are you still doing it?* & I said she should go first
because of her condition & she said you know what I mean
& for a minute I wanted to cry. Murphy said she looked like a
bridesmaid in her blue velvet dress & his words burned me
reminding me of the day of his sister's wedding when
I'd put the fear of God into Dora. It would have been
good to think I'd saved one life – even though Dora was still
fierce scared – if it wasn't a reminder of the other one.

73.

WHAT's worse do you think? asked Murphy. The existential angst
or the existential dread? & I said Can you have both
at the same time? Dora didn't even answer him now, her face
was round, the American eagle gone. I wasn't
coming back to college but Dora said she would keep studying,
Let anyone try to stop me! & there was a savage roar from
the other end of The Long Valley. A white-haired man in tan
corduroy & huge shoes was shouting about the Nobel Prize for Poetry
& a young fellow with brown curly hair was holding on to his arm.
Humphrey stood alert behind the bar in his white apron &
Murphy said, The poets are at it again! Are there poets in Cork? I asked
& Dora said, sure that's Jim Houlihan. Don't tell me you never heard
me talking about him. There was another roar & Murphy said
Looks like he won't be a candidate for the Nobel Peace Prize either.

HAVE you never seen the poets in Café Lorca? Murphy asked.
I only remembered being stuck in Café Lorca with a fellow
who said, *You'll find a lot of nonsense at the bottom
of a milk carton.* Houlihan staggered past & nearly got singed
by Dora's fag & Murph said he'd heard Carl had gone Provo
since he met Justin. It was true & Carl's Fine Gael TD
father didn't even make Justin mad, it made him very excited,
What does he see in her? I heard him asking Clodagh when I was
in the bathroom with my fingers down my throat.
Carl told Justin that Johnny Cash was in San Quentin for
murdering his mother-in-law & Justin said he didn't blame him.
When they asked Grandad for stories about the old IRA,
Grandad said, *John Redmond was a gentleman & they stabbed
him in the back!* so they left him alone, smiling to himself.

IT will be another life for you now, said Justin, his brown
eyes like drinking chocolate. *Thank God you saw sense!* I bought
two nurse's uniforms from the special shop, a wide navy belt
with metal clasps. I pulled it tight. Johnny O'Hare came
in wearing a grey, double-breasted suit, holding a bundle of VHS
tapes to his chest. Justin said, *She's finally off my hands!*
(After I paying for myself with the money from Larry's will.)
& I went red, remembering when I'd pretended not to know
Johnny but he winked at me when Justin said Carl was very
down to earth for Who He Is! Justin didn't like the wink, *Do you know
who Carl is?* Johnny said he did & could he have two packets
of Erin Oxtail soup. *He'll be the makings of her!* said Justin.
Time will tell, I squeaked but even Johnny didn't seem
to be listening. He just wanted his soup.